THE HANDBOOK OF HOSPITALITY MANAGEMENT

THE HANDBOOK OF HOSPITALITY MANAGEMENT

Arthur S. Weinberger

Copyright © 2002 by Arthur S. Weinberger.

Library of Congress Number: 2002096186
ISBN : Hardcover 1-4010-8494-X
Softcover 1-4010-8493-1

All rights reserved. No part of this book may be reproduced or transmitted in any form or by any means, electronic or mechanical, including photocopying, recording, or by any information storage and retrieval system, without permission in writing from the copyright owner.

This book was printed in the United States of America.

To order additional copies of this book, contact:
Xlibris Corporation
1-888-795-4274
www.Xlibris.com
Orders@Xlibris.com
16707

CONTENTS

FOREWORD 11
TABLE OF ORGANIZATION 13
JOB DESCRIPTIONS—HOUSEKEEPING 15
JOB DESCRIPTIONS—LAUNDRY 34
JOB ASSIGNMENTS 43
    Public Restrooms 43
    Houseman 45
    Lobby Person (Main Lobby and Ballroom Area) 47
    The Houseman 50
"HOW TO . . . ." 52
    The Maid 52
CHECK LIST 61
    The Houseman 61
    Bedroom 63
    Clothes Closet 64
    Bathroom 65
INSTRUCTION FORMS 66
    Lobby Houseman 66
LAUNDRY PROCEDURES 69
THE MARKETING PLAN:
    THE CORNERSTONE OF SALES 70
THE SALES OFFICE 72
PERSONAL SALES 73
TELEPHONE SALES 74
INTERNAL SALES 75
RESTAURANT AND LOUNGE SALES 76
BANQUET AND MEETING ROOM SALES 77
A GUIDE TO EFFECTIVE ADVERTISING 78

OUTDOOR ADVERTISING, DISPLAYS, AND
  COLLATERAL MATERIALS 79
PRINT ADVERTISING 80
DIRECT MAIL ADVERTISING 81
BROADCAST ADVERTISING 82
PUBLIC RELATIONS AND PUBLICITY 83
SELLING TO BUSINESS TRAVELERS 84
SELLING TO LEISURE TRAVELERS 85
SELLING TO TRAVEL AGENTS 86
SELLING TO MEETING PLANNERS 88
SELLING TO SPECIALTY MARKETS 90
COMMON LAW 92
LAWS OF CONTRACTS 93
LAWS OF TORTS AND NEGLIGENCE 94
RIGHT TO REFUSE/RECEIVE GUESTS 95
GUEST RESERVATIONS 96
CONVENTION/GROUP CONTRACTS 97
RIGHT TO EVICT 98
DUTY TO PROTECT GUESTS 99
LIABILITY REGARDING GUEST PROPERTY 100
LIABILITY/LOSS OF PROPERTY NON-GUEST 101
SAFEKEEPING FACILITIES 102
FRAUDS/TRESPASS 103
DECEASED GUESTS 104
LAWS REGARDING FOOD 105
LAWS RELATING TO FOOD SERVICE 106
ALCOHOLIC BEVERAGES 107
WAGE/HOUR LAW 108
LAWS AGAINST DISCRIMINATION 109
DETECTOR TESTS 110
LABOR RELATIONS ACT 111
IMMIGRATION ACT OF 1986 112
FICA, FUTA, WORKERS' COMPENSATION 113
TAX REPORTING REQUIREMENTS 114
GUEST REGISTER 115
CONSUMER PROTECTION LAWS 116

HEALTH AND SAFETY REQUIREMENTS 117
OSHA 118
LICENSING OF HOTELS 119
MUSIC COPYRIGHT LAWS 120
FIRE SAFETY 121
TAXES 122
WARRANTIES 123
ANTI-TRUST LAWS 124
FRANCHISING 125

FOREWORD

The author has recently written a book, *Anatomy of Healthcare Survival,* as well as, relevant editorials pertaining to healthcare.

The following is a "thumbnail" narrative on Hotel/Motel Management with the exception of "Housekeeping". It is known in the industry that the most efficient way to keep or lose a traveler is the effectiveness or lack of effectiveness of housekeeping. With this in mind, I have given that process an in-depth overview.

TABLE OF ORGANIZATION

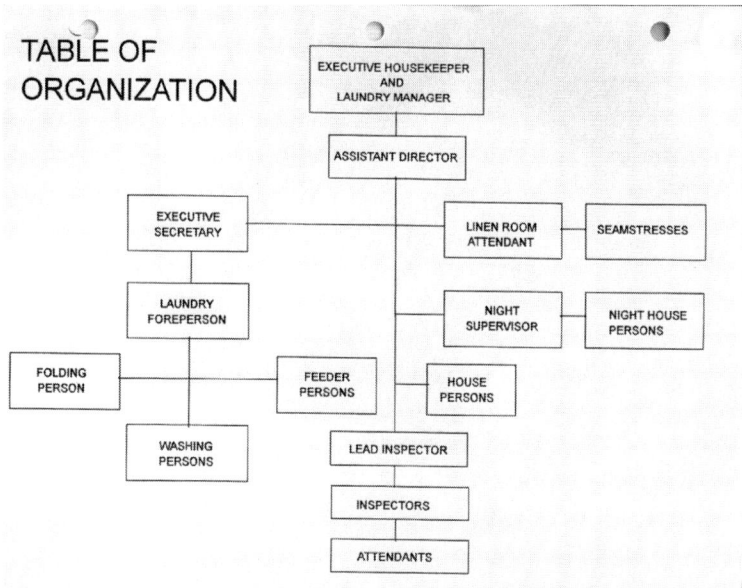

JOB DESCRIPTIONS— HOUSEKEEPING

TITLE: Executive Housekeeper

SPECIFICATIONS: High School education preferred. Six (6) years minimum experience in Housekeeping. Must have thorough knowledge for procedures and systems necessary for maintaining the highest standards of cleanliness. Must show the ability to train and organize staff to meet prescribed objectives.

REPORTS TO: Innkeeper

SUPERVISOR: Housekeeping and Laundry Staff

DUTIES:

1. Directs the Housekeeping program to insure clean, orderly, and attractive hotel conditions. Establishes standards and procedures for work and plans staff schedules to insure adequate service. Orders supplies and equipment, and investigates new and improved cleaning instruments. Supervises training and direction for Housekeeping staff.

2. Inspects rooms to ascertain that proper procedures are being followed.

3. Reports all pertinent information with respect to rooms or employees to the Innkeeper.

4. Must be familiar with proper procedures and is perceptible to ways to improve them.

5. Responds to all requests readily with follow-up.

6. Trains and re-trains all personnel in accordance with Hotel standards.

7. Takes daily inventory of equipment and supplies to insure that each maid is properly equipped.

8. Maintains a high standard of appearance among the shift by exemplifying such a standard of appearance.

9. Keeps a line of communication open with Maid Supervisors to give encouragement and exchange ideas and suggestions, and to promote team effort.

10. Reports all ready rooms to Front Desk, as soon as possible, on a daily basis.

11. Observes repairs needed in each room and submits reports on a daily basis.

12. At end of shift reports all rooms status to the Front Desk.

13. Disciplines workers and recommends dismissal of chronic offenders.

The above job description is subject to change and should not be construed as the only duties of the position.

JOB DESCRIPTIONS— HOUSEKEEPING

TITLE: Assistant Executive Housekeeper

SPECIFICATIONS: High School education preferred. Three (3) years minimum experience in supervising Housekeeping staff. Complete knowledge of equipment, procedures, and products necessary to maintain facilities.

REPORTS TO: Executive Housekeeper

SUPERVISOR: All Housekeeping and Laundry Staff

DUTIES:

1. Provides assistance to the Executive Housekeeper in maintaining the hotel in a clean and orderly condition. Assigns employees to specific tasks. Trains personnel and demonstrates new techniques and equipment.

2. Prepares daily assignment sheets of project work to be performed by housemen.

3. Revises assignments to offset absences of employees due to illness, vacations, etc.

4. Disciplines workers and recommends dismissal of chronic offenders.

5. Introduces new equipment and cleaning methods.

6. Inspects guest rooms, halls, laboratories, and other areas in the hotel.

7. Inventories and orders housekeeping supplies.

8. Instructs workers in cleaning methods.

9. Supervises distribution of linen.

10. Inventories linen to detect losses.

11. Responds to all requests readily, with follow-up.

12. Displays a personal enthusiasm in a job well done.

13. Maintains a high standard of appearance among the shift by exemplifying such a standard of appearance.

14. Keeps a line of communication open between the employees and management.

15. Performs any other function necessary to insure the smooth, economic running of the Housekeeping Department.

16. Performs duties of the Executive Housekeeper in his/her absence.

The above job description should not be construed as the only duties of the position and is subject to change.

JOB DESCRIPTIONS— HOUSEKEEPING

TITLE: Evening Supervisor

SPECIFICATIONS: High School education preferred. Must have a minimum of two (2) years minimum experience in housekeeping supervision.

REPORTS TO: Assistant Executive Housekeeper

SUPERVISOR: Attendants and Housemen (4PM-12AM & 11-7AM)

DUTIES:

1. To effectively supervise the 4PM-12AM tour of duty so that a high quality housekeeping standard is maintained in the guest rooms, as well as, in the public areas. Must handle all other relevant shift details, such as quest requests, in a professional manner, reflecting a continuity of responsibilities rather than two separate shift operations.

2. To provide adequate coverage for all guest rooms scheduled to be serviced on the 4PM-12AM shift.

3. To provide adequate chemicals and supplies for the Housekeeping employees on 4PM-12AM shift.

4. To train all Housekeeping personnel to the second shift procedures, including guest room and public area cleaning.

5. Inspect and follow through on all work accomplished each evening.

6. Report any project work needed in any area whatsoever to the Assistant Executive Housekeeper.

7. Constantly survey public areas, such as front lobby, and make necessary corrections.

8. Respond to the departmental beeper as required.

9. Report any maintenance problems to the maintenance mechanic on duty.

10. Report any operational and personnel problems to the Assistant Executive Housekeeper or Executive Housekeeper as they arise (attendance concerns, etc.)

11. Physical perform work when necessary to ensure a completed program.

12. Instruct workers in proper cleaning methods and proper use of equipment.

13. Perform all other duties necessary for the quality, economic, and smooth running operation of the Housekeeping Department.

The above job description is subject to change and should not be construed as the only duties of the position.

JOB DESCRIPTIONS—HOUSEKEEPING

TITLE: Housekeeping Office Supervisor

SPECIFICATIONS: High School education required. Light typing ability and diversified office duties. Maintains all documentation and performs clerical functions of the department. Effectively allocates the daily rooms to be cleaned to the maids on duty.

REPORTS TO: Primarily the Executive Housekeeper, though the Innkeeper will give direction to the position.

SUPERVISOR: Primarily the Executive Housekeeper, though the Innkeeper will give direction to the position.

DUTIES:

1. Compiles the AM/PM Reports at the designated time each day and distributes same to the front desk.

2. Acts as the departmental receptionist by answering all calls promptly and politely, and greeting all sales people and visitors in a professional manner, and relaying all messages as required.

3. Refers all maintenance concerns to the Maintenance Department, logging same in the Housekeeping Daily Log of Activity, according to departmental procedure.

4. Maintains accurate and up-to-date records for all Housekeeping employees including all personal information, date of hire, attendance, tardiness, vacation time, holiday time, etc.

5. Maintains an accurate and up-to-date Lost and Found Department, logging and storing all found items in the appropriate place as is departmental procedures. After three (3) months dispose of any unclaimed items per departmental procedure.

6. Carriers out any clerical function as requested by the Innkeeper or the Executive Housekeeper.

7. Makes recommendations to the Executive Housekeeper regarding problem attendance or punctuality for any Housekeeping or Linen employee as noted.

8. Complies and properly documents the Housekeeping and Linen payroll each week.

9. Carries out all other duties necessary for the efficient, economic, and smooth running of the Housekeeping and Linen Department.

The above job description is subject to change and should not be construed as the only duties of the position.

JOB DESCRIPTIONS—HOUSEKEEPING

TITLE: Lead Inspector

SPECIFICATIONS: High School education required. Requires minimum of one (1) year experience as an inspector. Assist the Executive Housekeeper in maintaining a high quality standard of housekeeping by keeping him/her informed on the immediate condition of all assigned areas and by training, supervising, and motivating the Departmental personnel to be sure all schedules are completed.

REPORTS TO: Assistant Executive Housekeeper

SUPERVISES: Attendants and Inspectors

DUTIES:

1. Prepares AM/PM reports for front desk.

2. Inspects all checkouts and releases to Housekeeping Office.

3. Has a basic understanding of the area.

4. Continuously checks assigned areas to be sure work is being done and personnel are following schedules.

5. Reports all pertinent information to the Executive Housekeeper.

6. Knows schedules for all assigned areas and is alert for ways to improve them.

7. Handles all requests with a sense of urgency.

8. Instills a positive service-minded attitude and feeling of pride in a job well done by the Housekeeping staff by demonstrating a personal enthusiasm and team spirit.

9. Trains and retrains Housekeeping personnel as directed by Executive Housekeeping.

10. Arranges for assigned areas to have adequate coverage at all times by checking the room status sheets.

11. Inspects equipment daily to maintain in clean condition and in good repair.

12. Answers phone with cheerful enthusiasm indicating a desire to serve, and logs all calls.

13. Maintains good public relations with all guests, hotel, and staff personnel.

14. Maintains close control on supply distribution and supply usage, noting inventory needs to Executive Housekeeper.

15. Maintains a high standard of personal appearance among Housekeeping staff.

16. Observes cleaning needs throughout the hotel, and submits written project requests to the Executive Housekeeper.

17. Correlates all input from attendants.

The above job description is subject to change and should not be construed as the only duties of the position.

JOB DESCRIPTIONS— HOUSEKEEPING

TITLE: Inspector

SCHEDULED POSITION SHIFT:

Mon.-Fri. 8:30 AM-5:00 PM
Sat., Sun., Holidays 8:30 AM-5:00 PM

SPECIAL JOB PREREQUISITES:

1. Must know basic housekeeping department procedures.

2. One year experience in supervisory capacity.

3. Pleasant attitude in dealing with the public.

4. Must be in proper physical condition to perform basic cleaning chores.

5. Must be able to endure prolonged walking and standing.

MAJOR AREA OF RESPONSIBILITY:

1. Overall cleanliness and maintenance of guest rooms in assigned area.

2. Check with each assigned section housekeeper to determine

the need for supplies. Insure section housekeepers are in proper uniform and name tags.

3. Get ready rooms for section housekeepers, inspect them, and make sure that they are the proper status.

4. Spot-check occupied rooms for replacements of supplies and cleanliness.

5. Check on new employees often to be sure they know what is expected of them, and that they are doing the job properly.

6. Training of all new hires (section housekeepers).

SPECIFIC JOB DUTIES IN ORDER OF PERFORMANCE:

1. Report to work in a clean uniform with name tag and proper work shoes.

2. Pick up time card, area assignment, and keys in Main Linen Room. Punch time card at 8:30 AM.

3. Always check with Linen Room Attendant for early make-ups or special request before leaving for the floor.

4. Check with your assigned housekeepers for necessary supplies.

5. Physically check all rooms marked vacant for any discrepancies.

6. Bring or call any discrepancies to Main Linen Room (Linen Room Attendant). At the same time check for any VIP rooms in your assigned area.

7. Check with housekeepers for ready rooms. Inspect them and put into the proper status. At the same time checking for

engineering deficiencies. (Work orders should be written, in the event a deficiency requires immediate attention, call the Main Linen Room).

8. Check with section housekeepers for Lost and Found items, and turn them into the Main Linen Room.

9. At 3:00 PM instruct all of your housekeepers to start their evening room check. (Make sure all slips are marked properly, if not, again it will be your responsibility).

10. Make certain no housekeeper has left any untidies before leaving for the day.

11. Keep records in your book of all work done in your area so when you are off, the relief senior will have an idea of what is to be done in your section.

12. Finally, make sure that the Evening Report in your area is done before leaving and all rooms are done. Turn all maintenance request (work orders) in to administrative assistant.

13. Accomplish all other tasks directed by management.

JOB SAFETY ANALYSIS:

1. Make sure when inspecting guest rooms that bedframes are not "jutting" out from under bed.

JOB DESCRIPTIONS—
HOUSEKEEPING

TITLE: Houseman (Floor)

SPECIFICATIONS: High School education required. Will train.

REPORTS TO: Assistant Executive Housekeeper

DUTIES:

1. Maintains premises in an orderly manner.

2. Light cleaning, such as, sweeping, mopping, polishing floors and walls, and disposing of trash.

3. Keeps maids supplied with linens; removes dirty linens from maids' carts; removes trash from maids' carts.

4. Empties hall ashtrays, cleans vending area floors and vending machines; does heavy vacuuming (moves beds, etc.) in rooms when needed; picks up trash in hallways; helps with special assignment, such as, setting up rooms, and any related work as required.

5. Shampoos carpets when needed.

6. Cleans whatever machine he uses at the end of his shift.

The above job description is subject to change and should not be construed as the only duties of this position.

JOB DESCRIPTIONS—HOUSEKEEPING

TITLE: Houseman (Floor)

SPECIFICATIONS: High School education required. Will train.

REPORTS TO: Lead Inspector

DUTIES:

1. Maintains guest rooms in a clean and orderly manner.

2. Responsible for cleaning/servicing of maximum of 15 rooms per day.

3. Accountable to Housekeeping Office in regards to guest room status.

4. Dusts furniture, empties trash cans, and arranges the furniture in an orderly fashion.

5. Cleans bathtubs, sinks, and mirrors, and replenishes supplies of towels and soap.

6. Maintain an orderly housekeeping closet and cart.

The above job description is subject to change and should not be construed as the only duties of the position.

JOB DESCRIPTIONS— HOUSEKEEPING

TITLE: Houseman (Floor)

SPECIFICATIONS: High School education required. Will train.

REPORTS TO: Lead Inspector

DUTIES:

1. Maintain premises in an orderly manner.

2. Answers guest calls at night (towels, glasses, cots, bedboards, etc.).

3. Removes trash, sweeps, and mops all bathrooms, and replenishes supplies (Lobby and Top of the Line).

4. Sweeps and mops employee bathrooms, cafeteria, and back of the house corridors.

5. Sweeps and mops Housekeeping Office.

6. Any special cleaning assignments.

7. Cleans whatever machinery that was used at the end of his shift.

The above job description is subject to change and should not be construed as the only duties of the position.

JOB DESCRIPTIONS—HOUSEKEEPING

TITLE: Houseman (Lobby)

SPECIFICATIONS: High School education required. Will train.

REPORTS TO: Assistant Executive Housekeeper

DUTIES:

1. Maintains premises in an orderly manner.

2. Light cleaning, such as, sweeping, mopping, polishing floors and walls, and disposing of trash.

3. Cleans men's and ladies' rooms (lobby and ballroom), and replenishes supplies.

4. Empties trash from front office, second floor offices, and vacuums all carpeted areas.

5. Cleans and polishes lobby glass areas and mirrors.

6. Vacuums carpets and cleans walls in the guest elevators.

7. Special assignments.

8. Vacuums and damp mops garage elevators and carpeted area getting off elevators at garage areas.

9. Vacuums both entrance ways on the outside.

10. Clean whatever machinery that was used at the end of the shift.

The above job description is subject to change and should not be construed as the only duties of the position.

JOB DESCRIPTIONS— LAUNDRY

TITLE: Laundry Foreperson

SPECIFICATIONS: High School education required. Experience required.

REPORTS TO: Assistant Executive Housekeeper

DUTIES:

1. Supervises laundry staff.

2. Responsible for the timing of all laundry for distribution to housekeeping.

3. Responsible for efficiency in the laundry room.

4. Responsible for cleanliness of premises.

5. Participates in all duties when work load is heavy.

6. Operates dryers, shakes clothes before they are inserted into the feeder.

7. Performs tasks assigned by management.

The above job description is subject to change and should not be construed as the only duties of the position.

JOB DESCRIPTIONS— LAUNDRY

TITLE: Linen Room Attendant

QUALIFICATIONS: High School education preferred. Must have the ability to read, speak, and write English and follow simple written and oral directions. Some sewing experience is necessary.

REPORTS TO: Assistant Executive Housekeeper

DUTIES:

1. Responsible for stocking and maintaining proper inventories of clean linens as they arrive.

2. Delivers clean linens to individual guest floors and maids' closets by use of the linen room runner.

3. Inspects linen for tears; returns improperly laundered articles to laundry.

4. Sees that tears are mended.

5. Inventories linen.

6. Collects dirty uniforms and issues clean uniforms.

7. Distributes supplies to attendants.

The above job description is subject to change and should not be construed as the only duties of the position.

JOB DESCRIPTIONS—LAUNDRY

TITLE: Seamstresses

QUALIFICATIONS: High School education preferred. Must profess sufficient skills in the mending and tailoring of uniforms and textile goods. Complete knowledge of equipment operation essential. To support the hotel by doing all repairs necessary on hotel linen, bedspreads, drapes, uniforms, etc.

REPORTS TO: Linen Room Attendant

DUTIES:

1. To make all necessary repairs on all hotel linen, bedspreads, drapes, uniforms, and shower curtains and any other items as requested.

2. To keep the sewing machine properly maintained (with oil, etc.) cleaned, and reports any malfunctions to the Linen Room Attendant or the Executive Housekeeper.

3. To perform any other duties or responsibilities necessary for the quality, efficiency, and economic operation of the Linen and Housekeeping Department.

The above job description is subject to change and should not be construed as the only duties of the position.

JOB DESCRIPTIONS— LAUNDRY

TITLE: Laundry Foreperson

QUALIFICATIONS: High School education preferred. Experience required.

REPORTS TO: Assistant Executive Housekeeper

DUTIES:

1. Supervises Laundry Staff.

2. Responsible for the timing of all laundry for distribution to housekeeping.

3. Responsible for efficiency in the laundry room.

4. Responsible for cleanliness of premises.

5. Participates in all duties when workload is heavy.

6. Operates dryers, shakes clothes before they are inserted into the feeder.

7. Whatever task assigned by management.

The above job description is subject to change and should not be construed as the only duties of the position.

JOB DESCRIPTIONS—LAUNDRY

TITLE: Folder

QUALIFICATIONS: High School education not necessary. Experience preferred, but not required.

REPORTS TO: Laundry Foreperson

DUTIES:

1. Maintains folding machine.

2. Stands at machine and removes articles as they come out of machine, folds towels, wash cloths, etc.

3. Makes certain articles are folded precisely for ease in stacking and for appearance.

4. Articles are stacked into bins and distributed to housekeeping.

5. Works as rapidly and efficiently as possible.

6. Maintain a clean area.

7. Performs any duties assigned by management.

The above job description is subject to change and should not be construed as the only duties of the position.

JOB DESCRIPTIONS— LAUNDRY

TITLE: Head Washer and Washer

QUALIFICATIONS: High School education preferred, but not necessary. Experience preferred, but will train.

REPORTS TO: Laundry Foreperson

DUTIES:

1. Responsible for the washing of articles including: sheets, pillow cases, towels, wash cloths, napkins, and table tops.

2. Determines cycle and amount of detergent.

3. When cycle is complete, removes clean clothes, and piles them in bins.

4. Determines wash load.

5. Helps in shaking of sheets when work load is heavy.

6. Maintains a clean area.

7. Performs any duties assigned by management.

The above job description is subject to change and should not be construed as the only duties of the position.

JOB DESCRIPTIONS—LAUNDRY

TITLE: Pillow Case Feeder

QUALIFICATIONS: High School education not necessary. Experience preferred, but not required.

REPORTS TO: Laundry Foreperson

DUTIES:

1. Maintains machine.

2. Stands at machine and inserts pillow cases into machine carefully, machine folds pillow cases and they empty into a pile. Remove pile of pillow cases.

3. Stacks pillow cases into bins for distribution to housekeeping.

4. Works as speedily and as efficiently as possible.

5. Participates in helping others when workload is heavy.

6. Maintains a clean area.

7. Performs any duties assigned by management.

The above job description is subject to change and should not be construed as the only duties of the position.

JOB DESCRIPTIONS— LAUNDRY

TITLE: Feeder

QUALIFICATIONS: High School education not required. Experience preferred, but will train. Speed and efficiency are important.

REPORTS TO: Laundry Foreperson

DUTIES:

1. Maintains feeder machine.

2. Stands at machine and inserts sheets, etc. for pressing and folding.

3. Shakes laundry before inserting for ease of insertion.

4. Keeps up with work load, maintains efficiency in operation of feeder.

5. Usually two (2) at machine.

6. Maintains a clean area.

7. Performs whatever duties assigned by management.

    The above job description is subject to change and should not be construed as the only duties of the position.

JOB ASSIGNMENTS

Public Restrooms

1. Wet mop floors twice during day shift and once during night shift. Spot-mop in between when necessary. Use small amount of stripper in water (8 oz. to 1 gallon water), with extra concern for corners and edges.

2. Refill all dispensers.

3. Wipe down all dispensers with all-purpose cleaner. Wipe dry faucets and porcelain sinks, toilet bowls, urinals and tanks with all-purpose cleaner, pipes underneath sinks, as well as, underneath porcleainized areas.

4. Swab out urinals, inserting swab all the way down drain to clean out any discoloration.

5. Leave an extra roll of toilet tissue on top of all tanks.

6. Wipe doors, overhead hinges, and push plates with all-purpose cleaner, entrance doors, as well as, door to toilets.

7. Clean mirrors with glass cleaner.

8. Empty trash and insert clean liner. Put 5-6 folded liners under the replacement liner so that you don't have to search for a refill constantly.

9. All vertical and horizontal surfaces are to be rechecked on leaving the area for cleanliness.

10. Recheck periodically during work assignment for spot cleaning and replenishing of various supplies.

JOB ASSIGNMENTS

Houseman

1. Deliver linens and supplies to their respective floors. Stock supplies on shelf neatly.

2. Collect soiled laundry and throw down chute. Do not stack in hallways! Collect trash and transport to compactor and compact material. Bring down soiled glasses.

3. Vacuum rug or wet mop flooring in janitorial closets. In conjunction with the floorlady maintain a neat closet and cart.

4. Vacuum hallways once daily. Damp mop with all-purpose cleaner tile area at cigarette and ice machine once daily being certain that underneath area is not cluttered and dusty. Wipe down cigarette machine and ice maker with all-purpose cleaner.

5. Wipe elevator doors and wall in that area with all-purpose cleaner twice a week. Clean stainless direction arrows above elevators with stainless cleaner. Dust venetians once weekly.

6. Spot double door as needed and clean push plates daily with stainless cleaner. Clean glass on those doors daily.

7. Sweep and dust mop service areas daily. Wet mop with all-purpose cleaner and four ounces of stripper, paying particular attention to corners and edges to prevent build-up.

8. Carry putty knife to scrape up gum, dig out corners, etc. during the course of your labors.

9. Sweep and dust mop one stairwell (both ends) per day and wipe down exit doors once weekly with all-purpose cleaner. Spot walls during stairwell process.

10. Dust corridor lights once weekly.

11. Wash out trash container by ice maker once a week with all-purpose cleaner. Wipe top daily with all-purpose cleaner.

12. Housemen will assure that vacuum bags are emptied periodically (usually when 1/4 full), and if they are malfunctioning to bring the machine to the office for tender loving care.

JOB ASSIGNMENTS

Lobby Person (Main Lobby and Ballroom Area)

1. Vacuum completely twice daily with large vacuum—entrance ways once daily.

2. Use lobby pan and small broom to police the same area when noticeable debris appear.

3. Move furniture to vacuum along wall twice a week.

4. Use porto-vacuum to get to tight areas.

5. Baseboards cleaned with All-Purpose cleaner once a week.

6. Gift shop door glass cleaned daily.

7. Empty trash twice a day.

8. Lobby glass cleaned with glass cleaner at both entrances daily. Spot cleaned periodically during day.

9. Metal frames and ledges cleaned with All-Purpose cleaner twice a week.

10. Urns policed when refuse evident.

Elevators

1. Vacuumed once daily.

2. Police every hour with lobby panned toy broom.

3. Use Posto-Vac along sides to clean any accumulation noted.

4. Spot doors, glass, and walls on an on-going basis.

5. Empty ash trays during "policing" procedures.

6. Clean ash trays at the same time.

7. Clean rope posts at Patio entrance with stainless cleaner daily.

Men's Rest Rooms

1. Men's room floor wet mopped twice daily.

2. Spot mopped when necessary.

3. Wash basins and tops cleaned with All-Purpose cleaner.

4. Faucets cleaned with same.

5. Mirrors cleaned with glass cleaner.

6. Toilet tissues, hand towels, and hand soap replenished periodically during the day.

7. Outside of toilet wiped down with All-Purpose cleaner, inside of bowl swabbed out with creme cleanser.

8. Same with urinals.

9. Door push plate cleaned periodically during the day with stainless cleaner.

Garage Elevators

1. Garage elevators dry mopped twice daily.

2. Garage elevator rugs vacuumed once daily.

3. Glass areas cleaned with glass cleaner once a week. Spot cleaned when necessary.

4. Metal ledges cleaned twice a week with All-Purpose cleaner.

Game Room

1. Game room floor dust mopped twice a day.

2. Trash emptied at that time.

3. Glass door cleaned once a day and spot cleaned in the early afternoon.

4. Empty vacuums twice a week. Clean outside of vacuum daily with All-Purpose cleaner.

JOB ASSIGNMENTS

The Houseman

1. Change into uniform, sign in, deliver linen, etc. to floors.

2. Clean drink and vending machines and all surrounding areas. Empty all trash receptacles in corridors and clean areas.

3. Sweep stairways and landings, clean railings, and wash all EXIT doors. Clean service areas.

4. Wash windows on EXIT doors.

5. Spot clean walls and doors, remove cobwebs, and clean fire extinguishers.

6. Collect soiled linen and trash from maid carts and deliver to assigned area.

7. Vacuum all inside corridors.

8. Replace light bulbs, as needed, in areas where maids cannot reach.

9. Assist in keeping all storage areas and linen rooms clean. Assist Housekeeper in checking supplies, opening cartons, and placing supplies neatly on shelves.

10. Report to Housekeeper any necessary information.

11. Sign out and change into street clothes.

Houseman is responsible to Housekeeper for supervision. Houseman absolutely will not be allowed to linger in rooms with maids at any time.

"HOW TO...."

The Maid

Housekeeping is the result of two things; personnel and proper cleaning supplies. The maid's responsibility is the development of a cleaning routine as is specified by the Housekeeper. There are many things to do in correctly making up a guest room. If the maid thinks of each step before she does it, she won't have time to finish the rooms she is assigned. That is why each maid is to develop good working habits and routines.

The routine which the maid will develop has been carefully planned by the housekeeper. There may be some things the Housekeeper wants done in a different way than the maids are used to. Keep in mind that there is a reason for following her exact instructions.

Starting the Day

Everyone shall report for work on time. (If an employee is unavoidably kept away from work or know's that he/she are going to be late for work, he/she shall telephone the Housekeeper). Each property has its own method of signing in or signing out. This is a simple way of determining each employee's actual time on the job and thus the pay schedule.

All maids should wear the same type of uniform. There should be a designated area in which the employees can change uniforms. Each employee should always be proud of his uniform. They should be kept neat and clean.

Equipment—Care and Use

The quality of any cleaning operation is dependent upon the quality of the equipment, supplies, and personnel. The equipment in use should be of superior quality. Daily maintenance is necessary in order to preserve the useful life of the equipment. A maid's job requires certain tools: sponge, spray bottle, johnny mop, vacuum, dust cloths of various kinds, and a maid's cart. These items are checked out to the individual maid. In order to get a replacement for a worn tool, a maid must exchange the old for the new. The other items used by the maid are the supply items. These are more or less expendable. They include cleaning supplies, guest soap, stationery, and other guest conveniences.

Maids carts and baskets are replenished each evening before the maids are relieved from duty. The carts are restocked with dust cloths, paper goods, guest soap, and special items, such as, shoe shine cloths, laundry bags, hangers, stationery, etc. Containers for cleaning compounds, disinfectants, room deodorants, and polishes are filled and the maids start the next day with at least a day's supply of materials.

Daily Duties

1. Change to uniform.

2. Sign in.

3. Pick up room assigning and master key from Housekeeper. (Daily room assignment will be furnished by the Housekeeper with necessary instructions as to check-outs and occupied rooms.)

4. Proceed to assigned area quietly.

5. Check all emergency locks before entering rooms on both occupied and unoccupied rooms. (If lock does not activate,

do not knock. If lock is free, knock gently; if no answer, enter room. Begin cleaning rooms indicated as check-outs, unless otherwise instructed by Housekeeper). Gaining entrance into a guest room for cleaning purposes is discussed in another section of this manual. Please keep in mind that any one using common sense and courtesy will never offend a guest. For purposes of these instructions we shall assume the guest room is a check-out.

The first step in the cleaning technique is the placement of the maid's cart across the door to the room in which the maid is working. There are two reasons for this: First, the Housekeeper can easily locate the maid. Second, the cart is out of the way of guests passing in the corridor and the maid has easy access to the storage facilities of the cart. The draperies should be opened all the way to provide working light. Turn on every light to be sure that all lamps and fixtures are working. Adjust the thermostat to the level designated by the Housekeeper. Put the room in reasonable order by removing newspapers, glasses, and used soap and call room service to pick up any food trays. Empty ash trays carefully as a safety measure against lighted cigarettes. Clean all chest and dresser drawers of any trash. Do not put trash or soiled linens on walkways or corridors outside of guest rooms.

6. Check rooms thoroughly for articles left by guest and turn in immediately to Housekeeper. Inspect room in same manner for missing furnishings.

Making-Up The Bed

Gather all soiled linen and waste from the bathroom. Then strip the linen from the bed, starting with the pillow slips and working toward the foot of the bed. Shake the linen out thoroughly over the bed to make sure no clothing or other articles are mixed with the linen. Should the bed linen, mattress pad, or mattress be wet, stained or torn, report it at once to the Housekeeper. Gather soiled linen in a bundle and take it to the hamper on the maid's cart. Be careful not to overload the hamper. The Housekeeper shall determine how and who should empty the soiled linen hamper. The maid may empty the hamper or a houseman may make the rounds collecting soiled linen from the maid's cart.

When the maid returns from depositing the soiled linen in the hamper, she should bring the fresh linens with her. She should stack the linens on a chair nearest the center of the bed. This chair should be convenient to the bath area, as the maid also has the bath linen.

How To Make A Bed

1. Smooth clean mattress pad on stripped bed.

2. Place bottom sheet, right side up, touching headboard enough to and both sides. Miter corners.

3. Place top sheet, wrong side up, touching headboard enough to turn over top of blanket.

4. Place blanket to within 6" of headboard, fold top sheet over blanket for protection, across head of bed.

5. Tuck top sheet and blanket, in same operation, across the foot of bed only. Miter corners at foot. *DO NOT TUCK TOP SHEET AND BLANKET ALONG SIDES OF BED.*

6. Position bedspread at the foot of bed. Center spread on bed and smooth out. Turn down at head of bed for pillows.

7. Place pillows, open end out, cover with spread, tucking spread firmly between headboard and mattress.

8. Smooth spread, making sure the bed is in place and both pillows are even and in place.

These steps make it easy to enjoy the luxury of a bed well made with fresh cotton sheets. This welcomes your guest to a sound night's sleep. *Linen must be changed daily.*

Keep in mind that linen is very expensive. The maid is accountable for check-out linen, as well as, soiled, pick-up linen. Keep all linen closets and storage areas locked up. Mattresses should be turned from side-to-side *weekly* and end-to-end *monthly.*

Bathroom Cleaning

The condition of the bathroom will spell the success or failure of an Inn's business. We must remember that everyone who stays with us uses these facilities and in doing so they critically inspect the cleanliness. Every bit of dirt or dust shows up plainly in the bathroom. There are the diseases that breed in all areas of human habitation. We must be aware of the danger. We must gain knowledge of how to protect our guest and ourselves from these germs. Careful instructions have to be given to all maids and other people responsible for sanitary cleanliness. Everyone must understand why certain cleaning procedures are necessary. Clean light fixtures in the bathroom. These are frequently steamed from the hot shower, therefore, they attract and hold dust and dirt. They should be cleaned with caution. Do not put a cold, wet cloth, or sponge on a hot light fixture. The bulbs may be removed periodically and cleaned. When this is done, clean the fixture at the same time. Exact cleaning procedures are given in the appendix.

The medicine cabinet should be opened and cleaned thoroughly. Clean the inside walls, shelves, and door with the 1-K Concentrate solutions, as described above. Clean any other recessed or open shelves in the bathroom in the same manner.

Clean the bathroom and vanity mirrors using Sparkle Glass Cleaner. Spray the mirror until damp; use a sponge to wipe dry;

polish with a day dry, clean cloth; and, do not use any glass dressing. The next step is the cleaning of the wash basin. Use the I-K Concentrate solution. If water drip stains are apparent, notify the Housekeeper who will see that the necessary repair is accomplished. To remove these stains and to periodically "whiten" the fixtures, use Bacteriological Creme Cleanser. This is available from Inn Keepers Supply Company. Do not use abrasive powder as cleanser. Use the I-K Concentrate Solution as it is not harmful to the finish of the fixture. Rinse the basin well, then with a dry cloth, dry the fixtures, and polish the faucet and handles.

The toilet should be cleaned next. Here is the point of real responsibility. Take care to use the following recommendations.

The toilet has two kinds of contamination. First, there is the human contamination and second, there is the contamination caused by insoluble salts which are present. The human contamination is the breeding ground for germs and the cause of diseases. The I-K concentrate solution, as prepared above, should be used to remove the contamination. This also disinfects. The seat, the outside and the inside of the fixture must be disinfected using the following:

☐ A fresh mint disinfectant which turns blue on water dilution.

These disinfectants are available from Inn Keepers Supply Company. The recommend dilution is two or three ounces (one-third cup) of disinfectant to a gallon of water. Be sure to rinse seat with water and dry well.

To remove stains caused by uric acid or insoluble salts, use Creme Cleanser. Follow label directions for use. Creme Cleanser should not be used daily, but only as the need to control stains and encrustation arises. Two cotton mops are supplied with each quart case or gallon case of Creme Cleanser. Pour a small amount of cleanser directly on the wet mop and swab under the rim of the bowl. The action of cleanser will remove the stains and encrustation which are nearly always present. Cleanser contains a disinfectant in itself. It will help prevent germs and odors by completely removing these contaminations. Proper usage will cause no deleterious effect on contact surfaces.

The bathtub or shower stall is cleaned in much the same manner as the basin. It is advisable to clean the ceramic tile walls before the tub is cleaned. Clean the walls with the diluted I-K Concentrate solution. Start at the top and work down. Rinse well and dry with a cloth. The tub can then be cleaned. The maid must dry with a cloth. The maid must kneel on a used bath mat or towel to clean the tub. The safety strips in the tub or stall will not be injured by normal cleaning methods. The tub is then dried and faucet fixtures and shower heads are polished with a cloth. The shower curtain should be cleaned very thoroughly every day. A toothbrush or the end of a very sharp instrument with a clean cloth around it will go into crevices where soap and dust accumulate and produce a black-looking surface.

If you have shower curtains, the shower curtain rod should be dusted daily and cleaned with a soft cloth. If shower curtains are mildewd, have a second shower curtain available for each room. Change the curtains frequently.

If the walls around the room show they need cleaning, this should be the next step; however, if not proceed to the floor.

In the cleaning and sanitizing of the floor use the I-K Concentrate diluted solution to remove the dirt. It is not necessary to flood the floor with water. Use sparingly and it will make drying time shorter. The floor should then be dried. The bathroom supplies, such as tissues, guest soap, fresh towels, and wash cloths are then put in place.

Look over the bathroom as a final inspection. Has anything been overlooked? Has everything been returned to its proper place?

The Bedroom

The maid should then return to the guest bedroom and begin the final cleaning.

Starting at the corner nearest the door, she should work around the room dusting furniture, window sills, blinds, tables, doors, and should end up at the starting point. Phone and light bulbs should be wiped daily with a dry, clean cloth. The dust cloth used should be dampened with Inn Keepers' Furniture Polish. Any wooden furniture should have the protective benefits derived from a coat of hard, lustrous furniture polish.

Check dresser and desk drawers to see that there has been nothing left by a previous guest. Check to see that there are adequate desk supplies in the desk drawer. If there is soiled or wrinkled stationary, plastic bags, etc. replace them with fresh stock. Check the closet to see that it is clean and that there are sufficient hangers for the next occupant.

The floor is the largest area to be cleaned. First, we will discuss the care of carpeting.

Carpeting must be protected from the wear of sandy grit. This is another purpose for "welcome mats" at the door. These mats remove a great portion of this damaging grit. Daily vacuuming cannot be overstressed. No carpeting will wear out from vacuuming alone.

To vacuum a room with the least amount of effort, begin in the corner farthest from the door. Some housekeepers may request that a broom be used to sweep dirt from the baseboards and corners before vacuuming. Move the vacuum slowly over the carpeting. Get under every piece of furniture with the vacuum cleaner. Then check to see that nothing is left there. At least once a week, the furniture should be moved and the carpet vacuumed very thoroughly. By working from the farthest corner from the door, you leave no telltale foot marks.

It is necessary that the vacuum cleaner be emptied and thoroughly cleaned after each day's work. A vacuum cleaner simply will not work if it is half full of dirt.

The final inspection of the room is most important. It shows you the room as the next guest will see it when he opens the door. Before the maid leaves she checks to see that the windows are closed, and fill out any room report. The maid must check to make sure of the following:

- ☐ The pictures, mirrors, lamp shades, draperies, and window shades are straight;
- ☐ There are no wrinkles on the bed;
- ☐ The pillows are flat and smooth;
- ☐ There is no lint on the floor;
- ☐ There are no hairpins, etc., on the floor;
- ☐ Every piece of furniture is back in place;
- ☐ Replaced any burned out light bulbs; and,
- ☐ Turn out all lights and lock the door securely.

The Housekeeper must personally inspect each room before it is sold. She must go over her check list to ascertain that no job has been left undone.

CHECK LIST

The Houseman

Here is a typical list for the maid to check daily before going off duty so that her supplies are ready for the next day and loaded on her cart. As she needs replacement of soiled linen, she should have the following:

- ☑ Bed Sheets
- ☑ Pillow Cases
- ☑ Face Towels
- ☑ Bath Towels
- ☑ Wash Cloths
- ☑ Bath Mats

Supplies should consist of the following:

- ☑ Stationary and Envelopes
- ☑ Laundry List
- ☑ Directory
- ☑ Laundry Bags
- ☑ Matches
- ☑ Shoe Cloth
- ☑ Soap
- ☑ Toilet Paper
- ☑ Kleenex
- ☑ Comment Slips
- ☑ Restaurant Menu
- ☑ Do Not Disturb Sign

- ☑ List of Services
- ☑ Glasses
- ☑ American Express Application

CHECK LIST

Bedroom

Mattress and springs in good condition.	_____
Mattress turned. (Once a week)	_____
Sheets tucked smoothly.	_____
Lamps Dusted.	_____
Light bulbs all 100 watt - minimum.	_____
Shades straight.	_____
Furniture in proper place.	_____
Supplies in place.	_____
Do Not Disturb sign.	_____
Pillows fluffed.	_____
Bedspread clean, smooth, and straight.	_____
Vinyl cushions on chairs being turned.	_____
Lamp connections.	_____
Door, passageway, or corridor.	_____

CHECK LIST

Clothes Closet

Sufficient hangers (6) Wood Type in Single, (8) for Double.	_____
Laundry bag in place with Laundry List.	_____
Shelf dusted.	_____
Wall and Floor clean.	_____
Back of door dusted.	_____
Shoe Shine Cloth on Hanger.	_____

CHECK LIST

Bathroom

Check face towels, bath towels, shower curtain, bath mat, bottle opener, clothes hooks, soap, toilet tissues, wash cloths, shoe cloths, and drinking glasses.

Are fixtures in good condition.	_____
Cleaned Shower Head clean.	_____
Water spray unclogged and the mixer is working proper.	_____
Hand rails and towel rails are securely anchored in the wall.	_____
The Door Lock is working.	_____
The lavatory drain open and free from clogging hair or lint.	_____
Bathtub drain.	_____
Toilet flushed.	_____
The bathroom is thoroughly cleaned.	_____
Mirrors and the inside of the medicine cabinet clean.	_____
The floor in corners and around tubs cleaned.	_____
Light and shade has been dusted.	_____
Toilet seat and hinges, bowls, tub, faucet, and exposed piping, tile, ledges, and doors cleaned and polished.	_____
Remove all cleaning clothes, cleaning material and utensils.	_____

INSTRUCTION FORMS

HOUSEMAN_____ DATE_____

LOBBY HOUSEMAN

	YES	NO	COMMENTS
MAIN LOBBY:			
Vacuumed			
Tables cleaned and dusted			
Gift shop door cleaned			
Men's room stocked and cleaned			
MAIN ENTRANCE:			
Doors cleaned			
Astroturf Vacuumed			
Trash and Sand Urns Cleaned			
SIDE ENTRANCE:			
Doors cleaned			
Astroturf Vacuumed			
Trash and Sand Urns Cleaned			
BALLROOM AREA:			
Vacuumed			
Men's Room Stocked and Cleaned			
Garage Landings Cleaned			
Garage Elevators Cleaned and Vacuumed			
MAIN ELEVATORS:			
Vacuumed			
Glass and Wall Cleaned			
Stainless Steel Cleaned			
Brass Doors Cleaned			

ROOM# _____ DATE _____   INSPECTED BY _____

ROOM OVERALL: EXCELLENT_____   GOOD_____ AVG_____
               FAIR   _____   POOR_____
MAID_____

	OK	REJECT	COMMENTS
DOOR VIEWER			
CHAIN LOCK			
DO NOT DISTURB			
DRAPES			
WINDOWS			
LAMPS			
100 WATT BULBS			
TELEVISION			
CABLE GUIDE			
COMMENT CARD			
AMX			
NOTE PAD/PEN			
GTD. RES.			
DIRECTORY SERVICES			
R. S. MENUS			
FURNITURE			
WALLS			
CARPET			
VACUUM			
BEDS			
CHAIRS			
DUSTING			
RM. DEODORANT			
1 LAUNDRY BAG			
8 COAT HANGERS			
2 ASHTRAYS			
2 MATCHES			
2 BARS SOAP			
1 SHAMPOO			
1 LINT MIT			
1 SHOE CLOTH			
2 WASH CLOTHS			
2 HAND TOWELS			
2 BATH TOWELS			
1 BATH MAT			
1 SANITARY BAG			
2 GLASS BATH & CAPS			
2 GLASS VANITY & CAPS			
1 ICE BUCKET			

STOPPERS IN TUB & SINKS			
BATHROOM FLOORS			
TUB			
SINK			
TOILET			
TILE			
CAULKING			
TUB STRIPS			
SHOWER CURTAIN			
BATH DOOR & JAMS			
TELEPHONE			
TELEPHONE BOOK			
HEAT			
REFRIGERATOR			
CONNECTING DOORS			
BIBLE			
CORRIDOR AREAS:			
DOORS			
WALLS			
CARPETING			
ICE MACHINES			
SODA MACHINES			
SERVICE CORRIDORS			

LAUNDRY PROCEDURES

Dirty laundry comes into laundry room and becomes the responsibility of the head washer and washer. They are responsible for the efficient cleaning of all articles. Articles are separated into piles and inserted into the washing machines. There are three (3) large machines and one (1) small one. The large machines handle sheets, table tops, pillow cases, towels, and wash cloths. The small one washes napkins, employees' uniforms, smaller articles, and leftover work that does not fit into the larger machines. When washing cycle is completed, articles are removed and placed in bins in front of dryers. All articles get dried except sheets. Laundry manager places wet articles into the dryers. Articles need to be shaken and placed into bins. From the bins, they are inserted into the feeder. Usually two (2) people operate the feeder simultaneously. The feeder presses the sheets and other articles. They now go into the folder. When they come out they are stacked and placed into bins for distributing to housekeeping. Towels and wash cloths need to be folded manually. Pillow cases have their own folding machine, and are inserted in one end and come out folded. They are stacked and distributed to housekeeping. Efficiency is the key to a successful laundry room.

THE MARKETING PLAN: THE CORNERSTONE OF SALES

Marketing is the foundation upon which sales are built. The marketing plan is a guide for the two primary means of selling hospitality properties—direct sales and advertising.

The Marketing Plan

1. Conducting a marketing audit

2. Selecting target markets

3. Positioning the property

4. Determining marketing objectives

5. Developing and implementing action plans

6. Monitoring and evaluating the marketing plan

A property can either directly compare itself with the competition and strive to compete "head on" for a share of a particular market; or identify a need in the marketplace and fulfill that need before the competition discovers it—that is, create a new market.

A sales committee is perhaps the most effective way to ensure that all revenue centers are included when setting marketing objectives.

Marketing budgets generally fall into four categories:

1. *Percentage of sales*
2. *Competitive parity*
3. *Affordable funds*
4. *Zero-Base*

THE SALES OFFICE

The most important part of any property's sales team is the sales office.

Vice President and Directory of Marketing and Sales—Considered the head of the sales effort at large properties. Usually serves on the executive committee of property.

Director of Convention Service or Convention Service Manager—Responsible for overseeing the servicing of group business once it has been sold.

Director of Advertising and Public Relations—Coordinate all promotional materials and establish in a good public image for the property.

Telemarketing Director—Manages the telemarketing center and works closely with the sales staff.

Market Research Coordinator—Oversees the development of information regarding the history and past performance of each account being solicited.

Listed below are some classic organizational principles that should be a part of every sales office:

- *Unity of command*
- *Authority commensurate with responsibility*
- *Span of control*

To build an effective sales team, the sales manager should be aware of a number of characteristics common to successful salespeople:

Professionalism	Motivation
Ability to communicate	Efficiency
Intelligence	Ability to analyze

PERSONAL SALES

A personal sales call is used to build rapport with clients or potential clients and sell them the products and services offered by the property.

1. Cold or prospect calls are usually made within a small geographic area with a minimum amount of time spent on each call. This is strictly a fact-finding or exploratory call.

2. Public relations or service calls are made on companies and individuals who are already clients.

3. Appointment calls are used to introduce a prospective client to the features and services offered by the property.

4. Presentation calls usually result after several previous calls. The objective is to have the individual, committee, or group make a decision on behalf of the property.

5. Inside sales calls are made to walk-ins inquiring about the property.

TELEPHONE SALES

The telephone can be one of the most economical ways to find—and sell to-prospective guests and clients.

To make a good impression and sell the property the caller must use good telephone etiquette, telephone communication skills, and listening skills.

INTERNAL SALES

Selling the property is everyone's business. Internal sales can be defined as specific sales activities performed by various employees to promote additional sales and guest satisfaction. The main objective of internal sales is to increase sales by promoting effective guest-employee relationships.

RESTAURANT AND LOUNGE SALES

Since hotel restaurants may have to co-exist with other in-house food and beverage outlets (as well as room service and banquet service at some properties) and compete with local free-standing restaurants, the positioning of each restaurant becomes extremely important. Why aren't more guests discovering and frequenting hotel restaurants more often? The answer is found in positioning.

BANQUET AND MEETING ROOM SALES

The catering department of a hotel can produce additional, often high, revenues and generate positive guest relations. The profit margin on sales for banquets often runs 35%, as opposed to 15% for hotel restaurants.

The catering department provides services for functions such as banquets, parties, and other business or social functions involving food and beverage. Sales of meeting rooms is most often handled directly by the hotel's sales office.

A GUIDE TO EFFECTIVE ADVERTISING

Two methods of reaching potential guests and clients: direct selling and advertising. Direct selling is a vital part of hospitality sales. Advertising can assist you by creating an awareness of the property before you make a sales call.

There are several reasons for advertising:

1. *Advertising reaches a vast audience.*

2. *Advertising is relatively inexpensive.*

3. *Advertising can create a direct response.*

4. *Advertising demonstrates a property's competitiveness.*

OUTDOOR ADVERTISING, DISPLAYS, AND COLLATERAL MATERIALS

Outdoor advertising, displays, and collateral materials are an important part of the sales efforts of properties of all sizes. Outdoor advertising is a catchall term that includes a property's sign, billboards, and other methods used outdoors to put the property's name and image before the public. This type of advertising is especially well-suited to motels because motels rely on passing motorists for a great deal of their business (two most common means of advertising property signs and billboards).

Displays are used primarily indoors to attract guests to the property.

For this advertising to be effective, it must be carefully designed and coordinated to reflect the property's personality and make the property stand out in a crowd of competitors. Outdoor advertising, displays, and collateral materials still play a vital part in the successful marketing of a property.

PRINT ADVERTISING

Print media, newspapers, and magazines in particular, are some of the most effective means of reaching potential guests and clients.

There are a large number of marketing arenas (newspapers, consumer and trade magazines, and directories are just the most commonly used print media).

Pre-designed corporate advertising that can be personalized for each individual property. This service saves considerably on the high cost of design, and provides guidelines for effective print advertisements.

In today's competitive market, this approach is often the most cost-effective, because chances are less that the property's advertising will be lost in a sea of similar, bland ads.

Small properties can make use of independent free-lance artists and writers, or small advertising agencies. For the best results in print advertising, keep abreast of the latest developments in the field.

DIRECT MAIL ADVERTISING

Direct mail advertising represents over 30%.

- *Controllable.* Direct mail is often called a "rifle" medium other methods of advertising which employs a "shotgun" approach.
- *Personal.*
- *Conspicuous.*
- *Flexible.*
- *Designed for prospect involvement and action.*
- *Easily cost-controlled.*
- *Easily tested and measured.*

Direct mail can be an excellent source of future referrals, rooms and facilities business, and repeat business. By using a good mailing list, designed attractive direct mail pieces, offering appropriate benefits to each targeted market segment, and promptly following up on responses, a property can build an excellent guest base at a relatively low cost.

BROADCAST ADVERTISING

Properties can use radio and television in conjunction with newspaper and magazine ads to reach more than 80% of the nation's population.

There are several factors to consider when selecting the radio station. Demographics, costs, a station's image, and special promotions offered by radio stations to attract advertisers will all play a part in the selection process.

Like radio, television is a saturation medium. Commercial television has a number of drawbacks that greatly limits the use of this medium:

1. General audience.

2. Decreasing viewership.

3. High costs.

One of the most effective uses of today's new video technology is property video brochures. A video can show:

1. Property facilities at their best.

2. A variety of setups.

3. Seasonal attractions.

4. Remodeling or expansion.

PUBLIC RELATIONS AND PUBLICITY

Advertising coupled with public relations and publicity can form a powerful partnership to reach in the property's target audiences. Public relations and publicity can enhance a property's image, good press relations are important to a property's public relations program.

Public Relations

Public relations program supplements sales efforts and is necessary for a property to compete in today's marketplace.

We will define public relations as the process of communicating favorable information about the property to the public in order to create a positive impression.

Publicity

Publicity can reach thousands of potential guests at little cost to the property. With publicity, the media provide the space or time, and the media—not the property—control the message. Publicity supports advertising.

SELLING TO BUSINESS TRAVELERS

The business traveler market is the fastest growing market in the hospitality industry today, accounting for over half of all hotel room revenues.

Business Travelers

Of all the different types of travelers, business travelers are perhaps the most knowledgeable and sophisticated, and they have definite preferences regarding the selection of a hotel:

1. *A convenient location.*

2. *Clean, comfortable room.*

3. *Room rates.*

4. *Recommendations of friends and colleagues.*

5. *Previous experience with the property.*

6. *Facilities.*

7. *Frequent traveler programs.*

SELLING TO LEISURE TRAVELERS

The leisure traveler market can be divided into two segments: individual leisure travelers and group leisure travelers.

Individual Leisure Travelers

Individual leisure travelers can be defined as non-business guests who are traveling independently rather than with a group on a pre-arranged tour. They can be divided into three general categories:

1. Families

2. Mature travelers (senior citizens)

3. Others

Group Leisure Travelers

Groups can be scheduled during soft business periods. A group is easier to plan for than individual guests. Group tour packages are usually arranged by a travel intermediary. The leisure traveler market is very large. Leisure travelers look for ease and convenience in travel and find special packages particularly attractive. Many packages designed for leisure travelers are sold through travel intermediaries.

SELLING TO TRAVEL AGENTS

The growing trend is that more business and leisure travelers are turning to travel agents for help in making travel plans and reservations, and properties are recognizing that travel agents and hotels make an ideal sales team.

Travel Agencies

There are over 30,000 travel agencies in the United States, staffed by over 200,000 travel agents. Travel agents book more than 70% of all U.S. airline tickets, nearly half of all car rentals, and about one-quarter of U.S. hotel reservations.

More and more, business and leisure travelers are turning to travel agents for help in making travel plans and reservations, and properties are recognizing that travel agents and hotels make an ideal sales team.

Types of Travel Agents

Travel agents can be grouped in three basic categories:

1. Retail travel agents

2. Wholesale travel agents

3. Agents who work for consortiums or chains

Retail travel agents act as agents for airlines, steamship lines, bus lines, railroads, hotels, car rental firms, and sometimes, wholesale travel agencies. Retail travel agents work directly with clients. Wholesale travel agents differ from the wholesale tour operators discussed previously in that wholesale tour operators work almost exclusively with group leisure travelers. A wholesale travel agent specializes in putting tour packages together for individual business and leisure travelers. Consortiums and chain travel agencies are associations or networks of travel agencies that have banded together to share information and take advantage of bulk purchasing and cooperative marketing.

SELLING TO MEETING PLANNERS

The group meetings market is only one part of a hotel's total guest mix, but it is perhaps the healthiest and most growth-oriented one.

Group meetings business can benefit a property in a number of ways:

- ☑ *Additional revenue.*
- ☑ *Ease in filling slow periods.*
- ☑ *Ease in employee scheduling.*
- ☑ *Repeat business.*

Types of Associations

Associations can be divided into at least seven general categories:

1. Trade associations

2. Professional and scientific associations

3. Educational associations

4. Fraternal and service groups

5. Ethnic associations

6. Religious associations

7. Labor unions

Types of Corporate Meetings

1. National or international sales meetings

2. Regional or district sales meetings

3. Training and development meetings

4. Distributor and dealer meetings

5. Executive conferences

6. Product presentations or launchings

7. Stockholders' meetings

8. Board meetings

9. Management development seminars

10. Incentive travel meetings

Dealing with meeting planners can sometimes be challenging. There are many professional meeting planners who are relatively easy to work with because they know the requirements of a business group. Other meeting planners are inexperienced. That is why properties that sell their meeting planning experience and expertise, rather than just their meeting space, will be the most successful at selling to meeting planners.

SELLING TO SPECIALTY MARKETS

International Travelers

One of the fastest growing and most profitable specialty markets is the international traveler market. Usually divided into three basic categories: North American travelers, European travelers, and other international travelers (Asian, Australian, African, and so on).

Baseball Teams

Baseball teams stay in hotels an average of two to four nights at a time, as opposed to the one-or two-night stays of football teams. While most football teams focus on group functions and meals, group functions for baseball players are rare, and most of the time players are on their own when it comes to meals.

Basketball Teams

When targeting basketball teams, it is important to remember that the average basketball player is well over six feet tall and may require an oversize bed, high ceilings, and additional leg room when meetings are a part of the team's stay.

Other Teams

Major universities and colleges participate in a number of other sports—hockey, soccer, tennis, cross country, and track. Many properties are finding the sports teams market so lucrative that they are developing special clubs that offer discount rates to teams and fans alike.

Government Travelers

One of the factors that has held many properties back in the government traveler market is the complexity of soliciting government business. Another factor is the assumption of many properties that every piece of government business automatically goes to the lowest bidder. The final decision is also based on the property's ability to contribute to the efficiency and effectiveness of government operations.

Handicapped Travelers

There are three main divisions of this group: the mobility impaired (confined to a wheelchair), the hearing impaired; and, the visually impaired.

There are two basic ways in which hospitality operations can meet the special needs of all handicapped travelers: removing physical barriers and improving the training of employees.

Other Specialty Markets

- Travel crews
- Movie crews
- Military personnel
- Sequestered juries

COMMON LAW

Each state through its court system develops its own case law and judicial precedent on issues involving state laws. Court decisions and statutes use the terms "hotel" and "inn" interchangeably. Various statutes define a "hotel" in different terms to accomplish the specific objectives of a particular law. The common law rules of the innkeepers' liability that apply to hotel guests generally also apply in motel guests.

Some statutes may establish requirements for motels that are different from requirements for hotels, usually because of the location, physical layout, and structure of the property.

LAWS OF CONTRACTS

There must be an offer, an acceptance, and consideration to support the information of a legally enforceable agreement. An express contract is definitely set forth in words, either oral or written. An implied contract is inferred from the acts and conduct of the parties.

A voidable contract is one which may be either affirmed or disaffirmed at the option of one or more of the contracting parties, but which is treated as valid and binding until disaffirmed. Statutes of limitations establish the time within which particular lawsuits must be instituted.

LAWS OF TORTS AND NEGLIGENCE

- A tort is an unlawful act done in violation of the legal rights of someone.
- Hotels and restaurants owe a duty of responsible care to their guests.
- The doctrine of *res ipsa loquitur* may be stated as follows: "When a thing which causes injury is shown to be under the exclusive management of the defendant and the accident is one which is the ordinary course of events does not happen if those in control of it use proper care, the accident itself is sufficient to carry the case of the jury on the issue of defendant's negligence"
- The rule of contributory negligence has been replaced by new rules of comparative negligence in at least 36 states. Under comparative negligence rules, fault is attributed to each party.

RIGHT TO REFUSE/RECEIVE GUESTS

The common law as modified by federal, state, and local legislation and court decisions still governs hotel and guest relationships and business transactions in the United States.

Under common law, hotelkeepers were obligated to take all travelers who applied to be received as guests.

The federal Civil Rights Act of 1964 supplemented the old common law rule by providing that hotels could not discriminate in providing accommodations against any person on the grounds of race, color, religion, or national origin. As noted earlier, some states also enacted state civil rights laws.

GUEST RESERVATIONS

- A confirmed reservation can constitute a binding agreement between a prospective guest and the hotel.
- If a hotel breaches a reservation contract, the guest could sue the hotel for damages.
- If a hotel overbooks, the guest may file a lawsuit, especially if he/she had a confirmed reservation.

CONVENTION/GROUP CONTRACTS

Each hotel usually develops its own contract form for reserving guestrooms, meeting rooms, banquet facilities, exhibit space, and services at the property.

Many details must be specified in any contract entered into by a hotel and a convention or group. It is important that a hotel seek its attorney's advice before entering into such a contract.

A hotel must review its convention contract forms every five or six years to make certain that they address all matters pertinent to modern convention and group planning.

Items cover in contracts with conventions or groups include:

- What the hotel is required to provide.
- Cost to the group or convention.
- What the group or convention will do.
- Payment dates.
- "Protection clauses," including:

    Impossibility of performance by reason of labor strike, civil disorders, etc.
    Cancellation clauses.

RIGHT TO EVICT

Before evicting a person from a hotel room, the hotelkeeper should first review the facts with an attorney to determine if that person is a "guest" or a "tenant". If the person has a lease, he/she is occupying the room as a tenant. If the person is paying room charges by the month and has been in the room for 30 days or more, check the local laws, because he/she may be considered a tenant. When a guest has overstayed an agreed number of days, the hotel has the right to require him/her to leave unless state laws forbid it.

It is important to contact legal counsel and the police in such circumstances.

DUTY TO PROTECT GUESTS

Hospitality operations have a duty of "reasonable care" to protect guests. Hotels cannot guarantee that nothing will happen to the guest. The hotel is generally not liable for acts that it could not reasonably foresee.

If the hotel is sued in a civil suit, the hotel should determine whether there was:

- Contributory negligence by the plaintiff.
- Assumption of a known risk by the plaintiff.

Under the doctrine of *respondeat superior,* the hotel is liable for torts committed by hotel employees in the course and scope of employment. Personnel should never announce a guest's room number so that bystanders can overhear.

LIABILITY REGARDING GUEST PROPERTY

- Hotels must post copies of required state statutes in accordance with the statutes' provisions in order to limit the hotel's liability for lost or stolen guest property.
- The hotel should exercise care with the guest's property from the time of the guest's arrival through the time of the guest's departure.
- The hotel may be sued for property lost from the hotel checkroom.
- If a garage on hotel premises is not operated by the hotel, the hotel should take steps to prevent its liability for property losses from guest cars parked in the garage. Tickets should be issued in the name of the garage.

LIABILITY/LOSS OF PROPERTY NON-GUEST

- A hotel's liability for the property loss of a non-guest is covered by the law of ordinary bailments.
- The owner of property is legally liable for any loss of the property unless there is a bailment. To become a bailee, the hotel must assume possession and control over the property. The hotel's custody of the property may be actual or constructive. In either case, the hotel as bailee may be liable for loss caused by its negligence.

SAFEKEEPING FACILITIES

Hotels wishing to meet a state's statutory requirements for limiting liability for any loss of money, jewelry, and other valuables belonging to a guest must provide a safe or safe deposit boxes for safekeeping of such valuables.

The hotel is usually required to post notices in strict compliance with the state statute to inform the guest of the existence of the safe or safe deposit boxes.

FRAUDS/TRESPASS

Crime against hotels may involve:

- Skips
- Fake or invalid credit cards
- Bad checks
- Theft of linens or towels

Knowingly using a stolen, forged, or altered credit card to get food or lodging at a hotel is a federal crime and often a state crime. Also, using a check to pay for goods or services when there are insufficient funds is usually a state crime.

The detention of a person who has not committed a crime can lead to civil suits against the hotel for the torts of false imprisonment or slander.

DECEASED GUESTS

When a guest dies on the hotel premises:

- Notify local authorities for removal of the decedent's body.
- Do not remove decedent's personal property until authorities approve. Seal the room if necessary.
- Take the decedent's property into safekeeping. Sometimes the hotel must do this because no one else is going to do it. A written inventory should be made. The task should be assigned to two or three persons to ascertain that nothing is taken. Secure valuable personal property in a safe.

LAWS REGARDING FOOD

Federal laws relating to food are contained in the Food, Drug, and Cosmetic Act which seeks to prevent adulteration of food shipped and sold in interstate commerce.

State laws relating to food cover the topics of sanitation, food storage, cleaning, water supply, sewage, and vermin control.

There are two theories under which a hotel may be sued for serving contaminated food to a guest:

- Negligence (tort theory) is the failure to exercise due care.
- Breach of the implied warranties of merchantability or facilities for a particular purpose (contract theory).

The Uniform Commercial Code provides for an implied warranty that food or drink sold is fit for the purposes for which it is sold. Food and beverages must be served and prepared under sanitary conditions.

Many courts apply the foreign-natural test to determine whether the restaurant should be held liable for guest injuries suffered from objects found in the food. For example, is a fish bone found in a serving of fish a natural or foreign substance?

LAWS RELATING TO FOOD SERVICE

A number of states have truth-in-menu laws. You should have on file a copy of any such laws in your state. Be certain to label kosher foods properly, especially when required by your state and local laws. Check your state and local laws if you are using sulfite preservative agents.

ALCOHOLIC BEVERAGES

Dram Shop Act makes the seller of alcoholic beverages liable to a third person injured by the buyer of alcoholic beverages. These are the usual elements that make the seller liable:

1. Sale of alcoholic beverages;

2. To an intoxicated person;

3. Who causes injury to a third party.

An injured party could also bring suit against the seller of alcoholic beverages under common law if that person were negligent in serving the intoxicated person.

WAGE/HOUR LAW

If a hotel or business produces $362,500 in sales for the year, it is covered under the federal law. To meet the minimum wage, a tip credit of 40% of the minimum wage is allowed. A "tipped" employee is one who earns regularly and customarily $30 or more per month in tips.

An employer must pay "time and a half" for all time worked over 40 hours a week.

The employer can use the cost of a meal as a credit to minimum wage if the employee voluntarily accepts it.

LAWS AGAINST DISCRIMINATION

- The federal Civil Rights Act prohibits sex discrimination in employment practices, that is, in hiring, promoting, etc.
- The federal Equal Pay Act generally requires that employees pay the same wages to employees who perform jobs that require substantially equal skill, effort, and responsibility and that are performed under similar working conditions.
- The Age Discrimination in Employment Act of 1967 prohibits employers from discriminating against employees who are 40 years of age or older.
- Race discrimination is prohibited by the Civil Rights Act of 1964.
- Affirmative action programs attempt to rectify possible past discrimination through implementation of a policy actively seeking and hiring minorities.
- Marital status discrimination is not prohibited per se by federal law, but it might be considered sex discrimination if a company rule affects married women but is not applied to married men or vice versa.
- Sexual harassment of employees by supervisors is prohibited by the Federal Employment Opportunity Commission under Title VII of the Civil Rights Act of 1964. Hotels should form a policy against sexual harassment.

DETECTOR TESTS

The Employee Polygraph Protection Act of 1988, prohibits covered employers from using polygraphs, lie detector tests, and similar devices, except in limited circumstances.

The Employee Polygraph Protection Act provides a limited exemption for "ongoing investigations". The exemption applies only if the employer satisfies rigorous procedural requirements for administering the polygraph test, and makes the following additional showings:

- The employee had access to the property which is the subject of the investigation; and
- the employer has a reasonable suspicion that the employee was involved in the incident or activity under investigation; and
- the employer provides a signed statement to the employee before the test which (1) fully sets forth the incident or activity being investigated; (2) identifies the specific economic loss or injury to the employer; and (3) states that the employee had access to the property.

The secretary of labor may commence an action against an employer for injunctive relief for violations of the Act.

The Act also creates a private cause of action by an employee or prospective employee in state or federal court to recover damages of not more than $10,000 for violations of the Act.

LABOR RELATIONS ACT

The National Labor Relations Act (NLRA) protects the right of workers to organize and to bargain collectively with their employers, or to refrain from all such activity. Two of the principal functions are:

1. To conduct secret ballot elections in which employees decide whether unions will represent them in collective bargaining.

2. To remedy unfair labor practices whether by labor organizations or by employers.

The NLRA forbids an employer to discriminate against employees. Violation of this provision of the law—discharge or other employment discrimination for union activity or other protected group activity—is an unfair labor practice.

Twenty-one states have right-to-work laws.

IMMIGRATION ACT OF 1986

- The Immigration Reform and Control Act of 1986 has made it unlawful after November 6, 1986, for any employer to "knowingly" hire an alien not authorized to work in the United States.
- If violated after November 6, 1987, will render employers liable to their employees or prospective employees.
- The INS has designated Form I-9 (the "Employment Eligibility Verification Form") as the form employers must use to comply with the verification requirements of the law.
- Form I-9 must be completed for all individuals who are hired.
- Civil and criminal penalties may be assessed against employers who "knowingly" employ an illegal alien or fail to complete and retain the identity and work authorization documents which are required.

FICA, FUTA, WORKERS' COMPENSATION

The Federal Insurance Contributions Act (FICA) provides for a tax upon the employer and a second tax upon the employee that the employer must deduct from the "wages" paid. The term "wages" is a broad concept and includes all remuneration for employment. Tips constitute wages unless (1) they are not paid in cash, or (2) the tips do not exceed $20 in any calendar month.

The unemployment insurance programs of the federal government (FUTA) and of state governments are related. While tax payments or employer (and employee) contributions are generally paid over to the federal jurisdiction, the state administers benefits under federal and state unemployment insurance programs.

Employers must usually post in a conspicuous place on their premises a Notice of Compliance with Workers' Compensation Laws (Form C-105 in New York), which advises workers of their rights and how to file a claim.

TAX REPORTING REQUIREMENTS

The federal government requires the employer to withhold income taxes from the wages and salaries of employees and pay these taxes directly to the federal government.

For the purpose of the ordinary hotel payroll, the term "wages" means all remuneration. Living quarters or meals furnished to an employee are included, unless such living quarters or meals are furnished for the "convenience of the employer."

If the total tax withheld by the employer from all employees amounts to more than $500 at the end of a quarter, the tax must be deposited in an "authorized financial institution" or a Federal Reserve bank.

Employers must furnish each employee from whose wages tax has been withheld two copies (Copies B and C) of the "Wage and Tax Statement," form W-2, obtained from the local Internal Revenue Office.

Congress enacted the Tax Equity and Fiscal Responsibility Act (TEFRA) requiring certain "food and beverage establishments," to report to the IRS the tip income that tipped employees reported to their employers.

GUEST REGISTER

State or local laws often require hotels to maintain guest registers. A guest register is a written record of the guest's name, address, date of arrival, and date of departure. Do not allow anyone to examine the guest register, unless you are presented with a court order or subpoena, or unless you have the guest's written consent.

CONSUMER PROTECTION LAWS

- Consumer protection laws are enacted to prevent unfair practices against the consumer.
- Plain language laws specify that consumer contracts must be written in plain and understandable English. This could apply to convention or group contrasts or catering contracts a hotel uses.
- The hotel must post the hotel's room rates.
- Some states and some cities have laws that require hotels and restaurants to provide no-smoking areas.

HEALTH AND SAFETY REQUIREMENTS

- State and local building codes often contain requirements as to capacity, exits, safety, etc., in private guestrooms, places of public assembly, and all other public areas in a hotel.
- State public health laws contain numerous provisions regarding cleanliness standards of bedding, sheets, and towels; the size of these items; and sometimes the amount of the item to be furnished to each guest.
- State public health laws usually require physicians to report every case of infectious and contagious or communicable disease to the health officer of the county, city, town, or village where the disease occurs. If no physician is in attendance, it is the duty of a hotelkeeper or other person to give notice.
- Health laws require hotels to maintain lifeguards at any swimming facility, whether a beach or swimming pool.
- The laws of some states and localities require dining facility operators to post, in a conspicuous place, diagrams, and instructions on how to aid a choking victim.

OSHA

The Occupational Safety and Health Administration (OSHA) is a federal agency to help ensure that employers provide a safe working environment for their employees. The agency sets standards, conducts inspections, requires that records be kept regarding work-related injuries and illnesses, and enforces the Occupational Safety and Health Act.

If operators do not follow safety practices, they may be subject to increased inspections. OSHA regulations require that by February 1 of the calendar year, the employer shall conspicuously post in places where employee notices are generally posted an annual summary of the prior year's totals of work-related injuries and illnesses from the OSHA Log No. 200. A separate OSHA Log No. 200 form must be used to present this summary information.

Hotels must also post a notice furnished by OSHA that informs employees of their rights and obligations under the Act.

LICENSING OF HOTELS

Hotels should also have their local counsel or hotel trade association prepare a list of the local laws and regulations applicable to them, and periodically update it.

Hotelkeepers in each community must also be alert and keep themselves familiar with the activities of local governing bodies. It is only through such watchfulness that hotel personnel can keep informed of proposed local legislation.

Most states and cities require a hotel owner to obtain an operating license. Also, licenses to service alcohol and food. Building codes cover the use of a building. State laws relating to food cover the topics of sanitation, food storage, cleaning, water supply, sewage, and vermin control. General health laws cover a multitude of topics such as water supply, sewage, reporting of contagious diseases, and purchase of dairy products only from licensed dealers. Laws governing swimming pools include not only building codes, but also cover the topics of lifeguards, rescue equipment, warning signs, etc.

MUSIC COPYRIGHT LAWS

A hotel or motel that plays live music or background music by means of a tape recording or record player or by re-broadcasting radio music generally has to enter into a license agreement with a copyright association (ASCAP, BMI or SESAC) to permit the performance of such music. Unless an admission fee is charged, music played on a jukebox is exempt from the ASCAP, BMI, and SESAC license fees, but a royalty fee must be paid and application filed with the U.S. Register of Copyrights.

FIRE SAFETY

Fire safety requirements are found in building codes, licensing laws, so-called multiple dwelling laws, public assembly laws, labor laws, occupational safety and health laws, sanitation laws, and so-called general business laws of the state.

The local fire chief should also be consulted regarding steps that each property should take to comply.

The Occupational Safety & Health Administration (OSHA) has regulatory standards relating to (1) "fire brigades" established by employers, and (2) the inspection and maintenance of fire fighting equipment.

TAXES

- Corporation franchise tax—a state tax for the privilege of doing business as a corporation in that state.
- Corporation income tax—some states also impose an income tax as well as the franchise tax. All businesses are also subject to a federal income tax.
- Unincorporated business income tax—those businesses not organized as corporations.
- Sales and use taxes. The hotel is liable for payment of the tax, but can pass it on to its customers.
- Hotel room occupancy tax. Sometimes it is called a bed tax. Permanent residents do not usually pay it.
- Hotels and motels which sell alcohol are subject to a special federal tax as retail liquor dealers. They are also subject to the regulations or the Bureau of Alcohol, Tobacco and Firearms, regulations govern such activities as mixing of cocktails, reusing liquor bottles, and keeping records. Most states also impose excise taxes and licensing fees on hotels and motels which serve alcohol.

WARRANTIES

- A warranty is a promise by the seller of goods concerning the quality, quantity, or ownership of such goods, etc.
- Warranties may be express or implied.
- Both implied warranties of merchantability and of fitness can exist on the same goods.
- Warranties can be disclaimed by the seller. The implied warranty of merchantability can only be disclaimed by specific language of disclaimer.
- The Consumer Product Safety Act is a federal law that prohibits selling any consumer product that doesn't conform to a consumer safety standard or has been banned as hazardous.

ANTI-TRUST LAWS

The Sherman Act prohibits a contract, combination, or conspiracy in restraint of trade or commerce.

Certain types of activities are always illegal.

- Horizontal price agreements: two or more competing hotels agreeing on what price to charge for rooms.
- Group boycotts: two or more competing hotels agreeing not to buy supplies from a vendor.

The Clayton Act prohibits specified activities. Where that acquisition may "substantially lessen competition" or "tend to create a monopoly".

The Federal Trade Commission (FTC) may enjoin:

- Unfair methods of competition; and,
- Unfair or deceptive acts or practices.

The FTC investigates misrepresentations in advertising, sales, and marketing that are deceptive to consumers. Penalties for violating the federal antitrust laws are severe.

It is important to remember that a hotel operator may be held responsible for the conduct of his/her managers or employees which is in violation of antitrust laws. Hotels should see the managers are aware of the antitrust laws and their implications.

FRANCHISING

Franchising is a method of distribution whereby a franchiser, grants to franchisees the right to conduct such a business provided they follow the established pattern.

The franchise relationship is based upon the franchise contract. The advice and review of an attorney and business consultant should precede any franchise contract.

The FTC rules require franchisers and franchise brokers to furnish prospective franchisees with information about the franchiser, the franchiser's business, and the terms of the franchise agreement through a "Basic Disclosure Document".

The use of the management contract has proven very successful to such major chains as Sheraton and Hilton as a means of rapidly expanding their operations with far less investment per property than direct ownership requires.

Under the management contract, the manager is responsible for the operation and management of the property. The manager usually pays the operating expenses and the remaining cash, goes to the owner.

Edwards Brothers, Inc.
Thorofare, NJ USA
November 19, 2011